THE DEATH OF DEMOCRACY

Written and Illustrated By Anthony W. Antolic

DEDICATION

This book is dedicated to all of those people who want the government to back off and get out of their lives. This book is inspired by the Fourth Horseman of the Apocalypse; as you read ponder this scripture and think about why, "The Death of Democracy," was inspired by Revelation 6:7-8 that reads:

"When Jesus broke opened the Fourth Seal, I heard the voice of the fourth living creature cry out, 'come forward.' I looked and there was a pale green horse. Its rider was named Death, and Hades was with him. They were given authority over a quarter of the Earth, to kill with sword, famine, plague, and by means of the wild beasts of the Earth."

ACKNOWLEDGMENTS

Now I would like to give a special thanks to all the people before me who fought against over regulation in government. Thanks to the good people at Oathkeepers.org for reminding those who take the oath of office to keep it.
Thanks to the Boy Scouts of America for teaching boys to become responsible adults, which is something that our public schools refuse to accomplish.

Preface

In 2008 a harsh reality was revealed to anyone with even half a brain. This truth manifested in the appointment of the man who has become known in the minds of many to be hands down the worst President that American History has ever known. In his 2014 State of the Union Address, the President who many only refer to as the Obamanation, told the country, "Tonight, this chamber speaks with one voice to the people we represent." The problem is that Barack Hussein Obama has proven to be a walking Constitutional violation in the 8 years he has been in office. In fact the Obamanation has been quoted by saying, "we need to be rid of the Constitutions restrictions on government."

CHAPTER 1
THE BLIND LEADING THE BLIND

Superior Intellect

I am sure that you have seen the Far Side Cartoon of a police officer asking a blind man if he was driving a car that is wrecked in the background. This cartoon is a satire against the blatant disregard for common sense that the liberal laws demonstrate in modern American culture. The

Americans with Disabilities Act or ADA goes overboard in interpretation more times than not. Why are there braille signs on a drive up ATM? Do the liberals think a blind man can drive by braille? When the passion of the masses overrides common sense, we tend to create laws that have no foundation in logic. Another example of government over regulation is found in auto processing centers across the country. The cars being processed have not yet been and will never be modified before they get to these centers, so a paraplegic will never drive them for employment at one of these centers: therefore no one in a wheelchair will ever have the job in the yard of one of these centers, yet the ADA regulations say that the restrooms must be ADA compliant, meaning fewer and larger stalls. Therefore, these types of businesses must waist money on building permits and the remodeling of restrooms that will never be used for what they were designed for.

We as Americans tend to think that just because we have the right to complain about the way things are, it is our right to change things. However, many times we have worked to change things to fix what we perceive to be an injustice, when in truth the injustice has not happened yet. For example any time a special interest group gets its way, another group has their rights stripped away from them. I have talked about how so-called Gay rights activists love to acquire many more rights than the average citizen. However, what about the right to use the restroom while on your break?

Here in Portland Oregon, the Auto Processing center at Terminal 6, only had 2 functional toilets for as many as 60 employees to use for a 15 minute break period that was until Auto Warehousing Company was forced by the city of Portland to remodel and reduced down to one toilet for both genders. Now I already talked about the condition that applies earlier in this chapter. No one will ever be authorized to go beyond the gate that is in a wheelchair, due to the nature of the work. Yet, a special interest group created a law that infringes on the rights of the Employees at AWC.

Patterns like this only create more problems in a democracy, due to the fact that a true democracy has no leaders. Even those who are elected tend to look more to the desires of the voters than the Constitution, which they are sworn to up hold.

I was recently introduced to an organization called Oathkeepers, who works to remind elected officials to keep the oath they took too up hold the Constitution, which is not always popular with voters unless the Constitution works in their favor. The perfect example of the voters not wanting the government to follow the Constitution is the recent Gay Marriage case that went all the way to the Supreme Court. If the Court Officers would have upheld the Constitution, the case would have never even seen a docket. After all the government shell make no law regarding the institutions of religion and what is marriage if not a religious institution?

The down fall of democracy has always been the decay of basic morality. If the people of whom the Democratic structure governs have lost their standard of morality from one generation to the next, the democracy becomes increasingly less stable. As a result a government that was once regulated by Natural Law has resorted to mob rule cloaked as a ballot box.

The authors and supporters of the Constitution understood that the success of this experiment in popular government hinged on the Constitution being ratified in 1787. The Articles of Confederation were already failing due to a lack of desire to abide by them, mostly in the

Southern States. The rift between the North and the South became so great that an attempted 2nd revolution broke out. We know it as the Civil War.

Grade School history books will tell you that the war was mostly about the South wanting to keep their slaves. That was never the issue, after all many business owners in America are still allowed to keep slaves. We know ourselves as hourly wage workers. It has always been more cost effective for the slave owner to pay the slave enough to feed and clothe themselves, then to prepare food and bedding for everyone in the group. In fact if you think about who truly benefits from the increasing popularity of the Socialist movement, an argument can be made that big business are the ones who really want America to become a Socialist structure. Think about it, if you look at the Socialist model of China, the workers are forced to work just to eat. During the industrial revolution, child laborers were paid for their work, yet history still calls them slaves.

While the western concept of slavery is getting beaten and never having enough to eat, we do have substantial proof that the life style of slaves in Biblical times would have been the equivalent to lower middle class America.

Many people seem to think that Joseph was freed by Pharaoh when the Pharaoh gave him more work to do. Let's get real! Who is the lease free person in all of America? The answer is the President of the United States, because the world watches him like a hawk. The Pharaoh told Joseph: "you [Joseph] shell be in charge of my palace, and all my people shall dart at your command. Only in respect to the throne shall I [Pharaoh] out rank you" (Genesis, 42:40). Please note that at no time in this statement did Pharaoh say to Joseph, "you are free to come and go as you please, In fact the

Pharaoh makes it a point to say, "I out rank you." Egypt was a military culture, the implication was that Joseph knew he was still a subordinate to Pharaoh; he just had more privileges than other slaves. Just like a Captain has more privileges than a Private, but the Captain will still get in trouble for going AWOL. By no means is the Captain or Joseph free to come and go as they please, they are both still slaves. In truth Joseph was even less free than a nameless slave in the salt mines, due to the fact that his profile was elevated and he had more responsibility. With more responsibility comes a shorter leash.

Misinterpretations like Joseph being free happen all the time. The more common the misinterpretation is, the harder it is to correct. After multiple generations of lies being taught such as, "Morality is in the eye of the beholder," the weaker democracy becomes. Religion and politics go hand and hand although people don't like to admit it. When we take religion out of government there is nothing protecting the people from government. Joseph got to where he did because he had credibility with Pharaoh. There were no special interest groups protecting slaves. As far as I know the Freemasonry was not a labor union. However, there has been evidence found that the Egyptians paid their slaves, contrary to what Hollywood says about it. In fact the slaves of Egypt around the 3rd dynasty were mostly immigrants, much like our Mexican imports.

Unlike modern America where illegal immigrants are being given amnesty, Egypt of the third and fourth dynasties, from 2675-2180 BC, would make immigrants government slaves, meaning for the most part a life time of hard labor. The liberals may want to give immigrants a chance for a new life but why pay them. Americans don't pay our prisoners so why take jobs away from Americans when immigrants can be detoured from coming to America by letting it be known that they will see no health care and if caught working unlawfully they well no longer be exported but be sent to the coal mines to work for free for the rest of their lives, illegal immigration will probably stop. There! The immigration problem is solved.

However, when the culture no longer adheres to the religion that they were born into the individuals of said culture lose their way. Let me tell you of a social terrorist group that I would like to call Mothers Against Dad's Discipline or M.A.D.D. if you prefer. During the generation of Doctor Spock, who called himself a child psychologist, an epidemic of teenage drunk driving was recorded and a few related deaths a long with them. This was also the same time that Child Protective Services was started to ensure that every generation to come would have a weaker moral foundation than the one before it. So in case you can't connect the dots let me help. Mothers Against Drunk Driving was started because a group of mothers lost control of their kids and people got hurt. If the time-out would have never been suggested and the fathers were allowed to discipline their kids and teach them to respect all of God's creation and not just themselves, we would not need mandatory Auto and Health insurance, much less seat-belts. Now let's solve the liberal problem.

Liberals are the downfall of every civilized nation throughout history; because they don't seem to have the ability to think for themselves.

CHAPTER 2
THE LIBERAL PROBLEM

Every great civilization in history has lost their footing due to one reason. In one way or another, they over used their resources to the point that their infrastructure could no longer be sustained. The Mayans depleted their woodlands of the trees to make the plaster that sealed all of their great structures. The circumstances in turn caused run off into their water ways and robbed the soil of its life giving mineral base. Likewise, the empire of Rome and even the United States, failed by over extending the empire.

Rome like America of today was too spread out. They could not defend their territory well enough to keep it. As I have said before, other factors such as morality also contributed to the fall of Rome. The first council of Nicaea was brought together by Constantine in 325 AD in an effort to keep the Roman Empire from destroying its self in a civil war. I would like to point out that in 325 AD, Christians would have been considered Liberals. I find it Ironic that even Rome was brought down to its knees by the destructive forces of the Liberal population. The two Christian sects from the East and West of the empire could not agree on doctrine and things had gotten violent, but Religion is not political? Whoever first said that Religion and Politics should not mix, needs to pick up a book for a change. For religion is in truth the political nature of Theology and it is religion that is the prime contributor to a cultures morality.

One of the most damaging questions I have ever heard is, "who defines morality?" Yet, the common school of thought is that morality is determined by the common consensus of what the majority of the people think is right or wrong. The problem is that many times in history, the majority has been wrong. So what then? It is for this reason that Religion plays a key role in human culture. It is for this reason that once elected an official takes an oath to up hold the charter or Constitution of the land they are being asked to govern, it is the charter that should govern over the elect and not the will of the people. Here are some examples of the grater majority being wrong.

1. Racial bigotry in the Southern States
2. Ethnic cleansing in Germany, Poland, Bosnia, the United Kingdom, the Ukraine, South Africa, and the list goes on...
3. Planned Parenthood Clinics only being opened up in predominantly low income black communities to control the Black American population.

Yet we give in to the pressure of our piers and so begins the downfall of the longest running social experiment in popular government the history of the world has ever known. Jefferson warned that Democracy fails, "if the population is uneducated and immoral." Such a statement may sound like a fear monger trying to get a rise out of people, but how can democracy work if the parents are killing off the next generation of voters before they are even born? So we have identified the Liberal problem. Now what to do about it?

I don't have any answers, this book is an attempt at satire, so with that said, it is time to blow some liberals out of the water. I seem to love to bring up Gay Marriage because it plays into the Liberal agenda perfectly. You see as I have said in all three books prior to this one in the Road to Salvation Series, the Democratic Party is Satan's Army on Earth. They never wanted the restrictions of a Constitution on government for with no restrictions they can destroy the souls of the American people one election at a time. Have you ever wondered why people brush off the fact that marriage is under attack in America? I believe that most people brush off these attacks on marriage because they don't want to think about God or anything that has to do with religion. But let's put the motivation into terms everyone can relate too. Let's talk about money.

I mean let's face it sin is big business in America. Pornography creates revenue for hospitals, the department of corrections and much more. The same can be said for drugs and prostitution. So what does this have to do with marriage? Simple, the Family is the child's first encounter with social interaction. Break up the family and the child has to learn to interact with others from other sources. Here is an example of how the government attacks Marriage.

One thing that I was worried about after Kansa and I got married was that our food storage had gotten low and we had to pay some bills that we were not counting on. In the fridge we had some bread and 14 eggs; we had potatoes and three onions on the counter and about 20 assorted cans of food. This was going to have to last two people for two weeks before we could buy any food. The crops that I planted would not be ready for at least two months and like I said, Kansa and I qualify for $16.00 of food stamps for two people that the government thinks would last a month. But the system is not broken? What a crock!

So come morning, I made some bread and prayed that my wife and I could make what we had stretch. Here is the sick irony that I hope people will appreciate, Kansa and I came into this marriage each having $200.00 a month per person. We get married and $400.00 gets cut down to $16.00 for just me and Kansa did not qualify anymore at all. Our income did not change, the only thing that changed was our marriage status.We have people telling us to get a divorce and just shack up to reap the reward of a socialist government who punishes people for getting married. As a result of our not wanting to give into the world's attack on marriage, Kansa and I are recording every challenge that comes up. Because for us divorce is not an option and we believe others would benefit from what we learned along the way. Before my wife and I got married Kansa was on SSI. But we learned that she would lose this so-called benefit if we made more than $2000.00 in a month between the two of us.

Here is the catch; rent without government subsidy is on average $800.00 a month without utilities and in some cases water. If you are lucky enough to have a washer and dryer hookup in your apartment, you save on laundry costs which averages about $20.00 a week for my wife and I. Kansa lost her government support the moment she married me. But the government is in support of marriage? RIGHT! Only if you're gay. At any rate just the move in costs of our first apartment, meant that

Kansa would have to get a Job, because I had to make more than the $2000.00 limit. The case worker also said that we were not be allowed to have over $300.00 in savings and that included my IRA. I learned than what the Welfare Trap was all about. The best way to not get trapped is to take another path, the Urb an Cook is a journal of our successes and failures walking the road to recovery from our addiction to government entitlements.

Our first move was to pay back the money that the government steels from each of us with every paycheck, to pay some fraudster, that has just learned to manipulate the system better than the other guy. It was to answer the abuses that the public inflicted on the system that started these rules, so I hold no malaise toward the Welfare system that Roosevelt started, just the people who run it. I was told all of my life that SSI was taken out of your check for your needs, so why does anyone have to pay back the money they used when they needed it, if SSI belongs to the individual? It is now my opinion that SSI and the rest of the Welfare System should be abolished do to unrepresented taxation. Anyway, now Kansa must pay these thieves $2000.00 that they claim was over paid. Just because we got married and the system is broken. By the way Kansa and I are both disabled, yet we still work full time and said F-u to Uncle Sam. I am blind yet I can still talk to this computer. With modern tech no one should be allowed to opt out of work. If you don't work you should be stoned to death rather than be allowed to be stoned.

Now I am not saying that all Democrats are evil just that they are following the majority because they are too lazy to think for themselves, and the leaders of the majority have very evil agendas. If you follow the voting records of the Democrat you can see clearly that no good intentions are ever seen from it. You see the Democrat is none other than the unbridled enemy to God, other known as the Natural Man. I spoke of this in Volume 1 of this series rather plainly. The bills that the Liberals are always trying to pass are clearly written with every intention to aid in the destruction of Man's greatest defense against Satan on Earth, the family.

Before my wife and I got married, both of us had $200.00 in food stamps a month for one single adult. As we got to know each other we pooled the $400.00 together, so it was easier for the two of us to have food for the month. However, on the day we got married, we both got a letter in the mail. The Welfare System cut Kansa off completely and I was only getting $16.00. Our incomes did not change. I was not working more and I did not get a raise. The only thing that did change was the fact that we got Married.

Kansa called up DSHS or the Department of Social and Health Services and they told Kansa, "you don't like it you can always get a divorce." Are you kidding me! We got cut off because the government does not like people who make less than $35,000.00 a year to get married.

In the Welfare Trap, I talk about several families who have had to find ways around the system and why. Kansa and I have found that working together for the common good of the family has brought us closer together as a couple. We both make our mistakes and we work together to fix them. When Families stick together, if one member is not disabled but still not making enough to survive, the government seems to feel that he or she would be motivated to get off the system if they gave him or her a push by reducing benefits, at least that is what the canned answer is when talking to an employee of the Welfare System. Unfortunately what the answer for many has been as simple as get a divorce and shack up together. This way there is no income cap for the spouse and the recipient gets the full Benefit. These laws were written like this to breakdown the family structure, no one can argue this fact. Yet if families in America functioned like Families were created too, there would be no need for government assistance. Therefore an argument could be made, that one of the things listed on the Liberal Agenda is to replace family with government assistance.

One of the ways they do this is not only through the rising costs of food but also what kinds of foods are affordable. For example, The store owners understand that American parents give into the child's demands just to shut the brat up, so the lower price is made up by sale volume, the ratio is 5:1. In other words, for every five cases of pop sold, the store may see one carton of milk going out the door. Our economy is adapting to America's addiction to entitlements and the entitlements are helping feed peoples addictions.

Another disturbing trend on the front line of America's war against poverty is that in many cases the parents food budgets goes towards alcohol, courgettes and other drugs because they know that the Taxpayers are happier to feed children than someone's addiction. In these cases one must question if the Welfare System is really helping anyone! For the past 5 years my wife and I have eaten comfortably on $50.00 a week and no government aid at all. We don't go to food banks or use food stamps, we just use what we have after we pay our bills. This is a fact that I am proud of. My wife and I don't go to food banks because most of them are government subsidized: therefore taking from a food bank is just putting a middle man in between you and the Welfare System. We will never take from a system that should be abolished!

When families make the choice of sacrifice to keep the sacred bonds that have made America strong from the beginning, those families seem to become closer knitted. The children learn that it is better to do for ourselves then take from others. The members of the family become stronger individuals which in turn makes the family unit stronger. The children from these families become more intellectual and less likely to give into the world's standard of morality. Thus they become better leaders then the children from families who are taking help from the government.

The basic reason families are under attack is simple. Man finds strength and courage in his family and the American government knows firsthand that the moment you stop teaching a child about the true nature of his nation the truth comes out anyway! The moment we stopped saying the Pledge in our schools to a flag that represents a Republic and not a democracy, of United States of a once free America, was the moment that our government realized that at least one father who was still loyal to the Republic would begin to teach his son what is needed to fight back, when the time comes. The first thing primitive cultures do when they occupy another village is to separate the men from the boys so as not to spark a rebellion. The children of Welfare Whores are not considered a threat to our so-called national security, because you don't bite the hand that feeds you.

Our government has been working to destroy families in America to prevent these words from coming true for generations. "[...] whenever any form of Government becomes destructive to these ends [to secure the rights of

Men], it is the RIGHT of the People to alter or to abolish it; and to institute a new guard" (The Declaration of Independence). At this moment these words written by Thomas Jefferson must be racing through the heads of those Men who have been working so hard to destroy our government. After all, at the time of this books first publishing, we were on day 11 of a so-called government shutdown and the time to over throw the liberals by force if needs be, would have been perfect. But how do we prevent these things from happening again?

Please Note: You can find the citations and research notes for this book in "The Note Book Magazine." You can buy the Magazine at www.ourcompanypublishing.com

CHAPTER 3
THE NEW GUARD

There is an infection that is spreading through the land like a cancer. Its symptoms are as followed:

1. An extreme lack of intellect brought on by having the same father as your offspring for the last 180 years.
2. A lack of work ethic due to letting the tax payers do everything for you.
3. Most that are infected with this disease are in some way guilty of the perpetuation of the epidemic of infanticide in America.

4. The infected hate or don't seem to like children, otherwise they would let them live. Most infected seem to have no preference between Steve and Marry in their bed.

5. You need not fear, for your dogs and cats are safe. Most of the infected are active members of P.E.T.A. But some of them know your horses a bit too well. Ironically they would sooner save a whale before their own child.

6. They are saving our planet by driving cars that are overpriced and become traffic hazards by taking 7 seconds to go from 0-15 MPH. But the Hybrid was a great idea. By the way no one knows how to dispose of the batteries.

7. They vote against the needs of America on a consistent basis. Yet they still think of themselves as an American.

If you exhibit any or all of these symptoms, you have been infected with the one disease socialism isn't trying to cure, there is only one answer. If you have been to a protest and think that you are doing the world a favor, run don't walk to the nearest voting booth and vote for the next Republican. If you have ever done a grassroots anything go to the nearest gun shop and register for your own hand gun and then tell me that our Second Amendment is not under attack. The truth is there is only one way to beat this infection. However if you ever thought Bill Clinton or Barack Obama, or even Franklin Roosevelt, ever did any good for America, I am sorry but there is no cure for this stage of this God awful disease, so take the gun you just bought and chamber a hallow point put it into your mouth and pull the trigger. Hey the Liberal is finally doing something productive. His decaying body is feeding worms, and now the world is a better place.

OK enough with the jokes for now at least. The fact is that America's political parties are polar opposites.

Although this book is an attempt at satire with a very serious subject, and the Democrats are the butt of my jokes, both parties are blinded by their own personal biases. As much as I would love for them to shoot themselves in the head, they won't, still the only way to prevent the liberals from coming back is to give them a taste of their own medicine. Besides if they all shot themselves in the head they wouldn't be able to give me anymore to make fun of, and as much as I hate the less developed of the political races, I do love to make fun of them. I mean come on let's get real, talking about an intelligent Democrat is like a Welfare Whore telling a guy that she is independent as she swipes an EBT card at the checkout line. The contradiction is begging for the world to make fun of it!

However if we are ever going to heal America we need to abolish all of the Welfare System and realize that the very concept of democracy is what is symbolized in Nephi's dream[1] in the book of Mormon, when he talks about a Big and Spacious Building with a party going on inside and the population of the building would mock those who chose to walk with God. This Mormon scripture is the perfect example of what happens when the majority is wrong. If government desires to destroy the things of God or undermine the sacred nature of the institutions of things such as Family and Marriage it is our own government that has become a threat to our liberty and should be cut off. For the sake of the next generation we have to do this.

Kansa and I recently went to a Islamic Mosk, to hear their side of the story as to why the Press hates them so much. The three men who I talked with pointed out that

---

[1] 1 Nephl 8:26 of the book of Mormon

Muslims don't drink or smoke. They pointed out that in America every thing is about money. The faith is under attack according to these men because the Medical, Alcohol, Tobacco, and Adult industries in America see not just the Muslim faith but all religion as a threat to their bottom line. It is these kinds of special interest groups who truly benefit from broken Families and Marriages.

The multiple generations of Welfare families in America have been taught to depend on the government rather than each other to help industry create addictive personalities. Alcoholism, Drug Abuse, as well an addiction to Pornography, seem to be well rooted in an addiction to entitlements. When a child grows up seeing Mom and Dad living off of the system and not even trying to go to work, they are likely to grow up to do the same.

Our children should be taught to go to work and be proud of the work they do. No one should ever say that you are not making enough or you are making too much. Families should be taken care of and not ripped apart by Social Services, CPS or any number of parasitic Zygotes with in the government. We must remember that the government existed to serve the people and not the other way around.

The Welfare System is failing because there are not enough contributors and too many clients. The Government shutdown should have shown us that we don't need a government that is so big. The world has not come to an end just because a group of employees who should be fired can't agree. We should use this time to clean house. The government uses the term government shutdown to intimidate us. However they should be the ones who are intimidated, they work for us.

CHAPTER 4
THE BLUFF

In this chapter I want to make one thing crystal clear, "there is no such thing as an unpopular government." We must remember governments only exist by the consent of the governed. If the people don't like what is happening with in the government something is ether changed or is abolished. With that said, Thomas Jefferson writes:

"[To secure the God given rights of the people] Governments are instituted among Men, deriving their just powers from the consent of the governed. [However] whenever any form of Government becomes destructive of these ends, it is the Right of the governed to alter {through election} or to abolish it {through Revolution}" (The Declaration of Independence).

We as Americans have become conditioned into complacency, to such a point that people seem to believe that just because it is the government who is screwing us, we can't do anything about it. Well this could not be further from the truth. If we get enough people together we could overturn the abominable INFERIOR {sorry} Supreme Court rulings, such as Row Verses Wade and Gay Marriage. I know, people have been protesting Row verses Wade ever since the ruling was made. But I am not talking about protesting, I am talking about civil disobedience that is organized on a national scale. If we hit the government where it hurts the most and remind them that they work for us in the process, they would have to listen.

Ironically, due to the fact that the Declaration of Independence is the first legal document that any elected members of the American government has ever signed, any laws that have been instated after the fact are inconsequential to your legal defense if charges are pressed, you see America's Justice System is based on this wonderful thing call Precedent. Law is a mutually agreed contract between the governed people and the elected buffoons, who for the most part choose not to up hold their end of the bargain. If either party violates that contract the law has repercussions for its violation or the contract is rendered obsolete, in which case why bother with the contract in the first place? In the case of the American government refusing to do its job: the employer {the Tax payer} reserves the right to abolish the contract according to the Declaration of Independence and put in its place a new guard to secure the God given rights of the governed.

The US Government has become too cocky, thinking that nothing would happen if they decided not to go to work one day. But here's the thing, Congress had shut down the government for 11 days and we are still here. All they did in my mind is prove to the American people that we don't need them. I have been speaking out against social programs all of my life, so Welfare checks not being cut would be an answer to my prayers. Bring it on you liberal scum. Prove to all of us how non-essential you all are. I think the next budget cuts should start with Government payrolls, let's begin at 1600 Pennsylvania Avenue. So guys I am calling your bluff. I propose that for every minute you can't agree on a budget, your staff has $1000.00 deducted from your budget. I say that all elected officials shall be mandated to live off of the bare minimum that the Welfare system allows. We shall see then how long the system will still be broken.

I say no one pays taxes until these changes happen after all a government cannot exist without the consent of the governed. We must always remember the government works for us {the Tax Payer} and not the other way around! I say considering the fact that the bulk of the tax budget for next year is coming from the faithful church goers something tells me that the courts will appeal anything we tell them too. After all it was money that bought Abortion and Gay Marriages favorable rulings in the first place. But most liberals don't pay taxes, so money come from? [...] exactly! Most of the liberal voters if not all are on some kind of government assistance. So let's hold the government's pocketbook hostage until the rulings get overturned.

You see democracy always fails when morality is lost. Our economy suffers when people can no longer trust each other. When human life is reduced to a price tag on a video game, it becomes very difficult to sell anything. After all, how can you trust people when you put yourself on alert the moment any one walks passed. For that matter, how can anyone trust our government when they don't even follow the rules that they set up for us. Make no mistake my friends, I am not saying that we need to overrun Washington with guns and violence, for this is a government that was meant to be under God but has giving way to the selfish demand of Mob rule, which is what Satan has always wanted. We all need a Revolution of Heart not a democracy.

CHAPTER 5
REVOLUTION OF HEART

In my researching my 3rd book of the Agenda series, I took Kansa to visit a local Mosk. The visit was quite educational. To begin, the word Islam means to submit. The dogma is similar to the Christians. But what impressed me is the fact that all four of the men who took the time to give us a guided tour of Islam, had figured out why not just the Muslim faith is under attack by the press, but any religion in general. They supported my thesis by explaining how all religions tend to elevate the woman as the sacred vessel of God's creation. But industry wants to take advantage of the fact that, "Sex Sells." As I said earlier, "sin is big business in America and the rest of the western world."

In the Book of Daniel, Nebuchadnezzar dreamed of a statuesque image of a man with a gold head, silver arms and chest, a bronze mid-drift, iron legs and clay and iron feet. The feet were a symbol of a fractured Roman empire that was literally ripped apart by the collective sins of their population. When governments can't stop fighting among themselves the stability of said government is doomed to fail.

I was invited to a seminar at a Seventh Day Adventists church in Vancouver Washington, I came in thinking that I would hear Dr. Roger Walter debunking the Rapture Doctrine, and in many ways he did. But He ended his talk with an even more important statement that I was not expecting. Dr. Walter said, "Putting aside your beliefs about the Rapture doctrine, what is really important is that Christ is coming."

It seems to me that the political parties of America could learn something from Dr. Walter's statement. For what really matters is the best interest of the American people. Historians claim that the clay and iron feet of the statue in Nebuchadarenezzar's dream is likely to represent the fractured remnants of the once great Roman Empire, who could no longer get along with each other and today by Italy, Germany, the United Kingdom, and several others in between.

Modern America could learn a great deal from studying the past attempts at democracy. You see every government runs its course. The problem with a government with no true leadership is that no one is willing to take responsibility when things go wrong. These days Men are having problems when it comes to trusting each other and why not, The Moral standard has fallen to the point that robberies are happening in broad day light and no one does anything to try and help.

When Men can't trust each other it is increasingly hard to Love your neighbor. As a result of this lack of trust not to mention love the governed lose faith in the Democracy, making claims that their vote doesn't matter: because the powers that be will instate who they want anyway. The lack of faith in the electoral system can ultimately lead to Anarchy. Such Anarchy begins with a rejection of the National Religion which I have talked about in great detail in the last three books of this series. The rejection of religion at a cultural level allows morality to fail. The loss of morality has led to such a Deadlock in Congress that the government gets shut down.

When religious issues such as Marriage and Abortion are allowed to become the platforms for the election of America's next Presidential Candidates, it should be time for the Voters to ask, what happened to the separation of Church and State. The first amendment of the Bill of Rights says that, **"Congress shall make no law** respecting an establishment of religion." Therefore, the involvement of any elected official or even courts involvement in marriage issues or any issues involving family, at all, is unconstitutional. There is no room for interpretation regarding a statement such as, "shall make **no** law," it is black and white.

Everything that is said in this or any other book that I have or will wright was once protected by the First Amendment's Freedom of Speech clause: Now with that said I hold myself in absolute and utter contempt to the United States Federal Supreme Court of 1972, whose paid political decision is responsible for the countless counts of infanticide, making the United States Federal Supreme Court of 1972 just as responsible for those murders as the parents.

If America is going to survive, we must restore the Republic. Democracy was tried and failed in the events that led up to the failing of the Articles of Confederation. Ben Franklin said that the Founding Fathers gave us, "a Republic, if we can keep it." The Founding Fathers understood that, "the limits that the Constitution puts on government would only be upheld as long as the sheep did not get spooked." (The Freemasons). They knew that the ultimate downfall of popular government has always been a scared mob that has replaced all reason with childish emotion.

For the most part our economy is based on the emotional responses of the population. A healthy economy is based on the confidence the public has in our leaders as well as how well the population can responsibly control our own personal spending. When more money is being spent on personal vices that offer no benefit to our domestic production, the local economy becomes stagnant and yet the majority made these vices legal. As a result democracy becomes the villein.

It is my personal belief that Hamilton's greatest fear for America was that "a democracy can only be limited by those who wish to impose the limits, but ultimately any limits imposed will be rendered void by the fore mentioned democracy, whose ultimate goal is always Anarchy" (Marcus Aurelius).

America is not too far from the Anarchy that many of the Founding Fathers dreaded. You see many have lost faith in the election process. The government seems to do as it wishes even against the will of their constituents. As a result of the abuse of power, laws are being instated to undermine the strength of the family Unit. Obama-care well be, as is any law that has to do with the Child Protective Services or the Education of our children, in violation of the First Amendment's separation of church and state clause, for the family is a Religious institution through Marriage. In other words, even our public schools and the existence of the Department of Education as well as Child Protective Services, are violations of the Bill of Rights! Check mate...

I know you are probably thinking that I am going too far in my interpretation but let me explain. Religion is instituted for the benefit of the education of our children; in fact outside of Row vs. Wade and Gay Marriage [...] well forget that! There are no laws that can't be rooting back to the welfare of the family, outside of those two. Even the annoying seat-belt laws that I feel have gone too far are there to regulate over irresponsible parents.

Our Founding Fathers foresaw a threat in a movement that was then known as the anti-Constitutionalist, who would later become known as [...] well just read the quote. "A Democrat is a political vermin who is only willing to follow rules if it suites him, therefore a Democrat has no perceived desire to uphold the Constitution which is the law of the land. The Democrat is first and foremost a domestic threat to the rights and liberties of our new Nation and should not be treated as anything more than a Zealot in the Holy Land." (Freemasons). Alexander

Hamilton felt that, "if these vermin [the Democrats] are not dealt with their selfish nature and hunger for power would squash the Rights and liberties that our families have suffered so many losses to keep, their sacrifices would be for not."

In my house growing up the word "democrat" was more profane than any of the four letter words I may have used. I could call someone a bastard and as long as no one knew who his father was I was fine, but if I called someone a Democrat I was peeling a truck load of potatoes for the restaurant. So it became important to me to understand why the word was so bad in the minds of the Nash Men.

Bring um in!

Much of a person's political preference has more to do with tradition than the issues. My Grandfather backing up a dump-truck full of potatoes for me to peel, was a hard lesson, but I was told another story that was equally as powerful.

A coworker of mine was wondering why his wife always cut off the end of the pot-roast, so he asked her.

She did not know so she asked her mother who taught her how to cook. Her mother did not know. Finally my co-workers wife asked her Grandmother. Grandma told her, "My dear you don't need to cut off the ends, I taught your mom to do it that way because the pan was too small, the roast didn't fit in the pan." Many traditions we keep because of good reasons but others we keep because we don't know any better.

More times than not people tend to go off of what they are told, rather than finding out for themselves. As an example, I was at work one day and we were told to move some product: however too many people were talking and I heard someone say, "Take it in the shop." Without finding out for myself, I took the product into the shop. I got reprimanded for it and rightfully so. Because even though I was wrong people followed my lead and the mistake costed us time.

These same kinds of habits we practice tend to be practiced among Men regarding both Politics and Religion. In all three cases nothing was done to check the facts. With Religion, people tend to want to believe the way they were raised, the same goes for politics.

Most voters will admit that they belong to the same political party that their parents did before them, due to a sense of tradition. However, the same people will not tell me why they voted the way they did on the issues much less what the issues is that they voted on. The Bible says, **"Study to show yourself approved"** (2 Timothy 2:15). If you don't have time to study the issues, don't vote! A reckless voter is far worse than a nonvoter, for the reckless voter is likely to get caught up in the passion of the Mob and vote in the direction they want him to. In fact I think the press should stop covering an election about six months before it is held so the media bias can be counter acted. People say it is your civic duty to vote. I say it is only your civic duty to make an informed responsible vote. Tomas Jefferson was correct in saying, "Democracy can only work if the people can remain educated."

The same goes for your faith. Too many people have died over things they believed the scriptures say but it turns out the phrase known as the Verse of the Sword is not even a part of the Koran. Yet Muslim extremists cite the phrase to justify their acts. Like it or not you can have religion without politics but you can't have politics without religion.

The religious traditions of a culture dictate the political direction that the culture will head in the future. After all the moral platform on which most candidates run is deeply rooted in cultural biases which has their roots in the local religion.

We as humans are not wired to compartmentalize one part of our life from another. Therefore it is foolish to assume the just because the Supreme Court says that we can't mix Religion and Politics, that it is even possible for humans to do so.

In fact we need only to take a good look around to notice that our American way of life is giving way to Socialism and ultimately anarchy. To keep this from happening we need to revive the importance of Family to our youth. We need to kick the government out of our homes and invite God back in. If American Democracy is going to live, we must restore a general sense of Morality in our culture. We must keep in mind that, "No power is given to you, except by God" (Romans 13:1), therefore if our leaders are not doing God's will, we must realizes that they have no authority left.

We must remember, law is a mutually agreed contract between the governed people and the elected buffoons, who for the most part, choose not to uphold their end of the bargain. If either party violates that contract the law has repercussions for its violation or the contract is rendered obsolete, in which case why bother with the contract in the first place? In the case of the American government refusing to do its job and up hold the Constitution which protects the rights of the individual, the employer {the Tax payer} reserves the right to abolish our government and put in its place a new guard to secure the God given rights of the governed. In the perfect government, no elected officer would ever be paid for service, but rather receive the same so-called benefits as those who are on government assistance. Something tells me that the government would stop attacking family if it applies to them.

Please consider this, the Taxpayers are paying for both the wages of these crooks and the crooks that try to take advantage of the Welfare System, but the Welfare recipients can't give themselves a raise. Wouldn't it be better stewardship of American taxes to just pay every one under the same umbrella? I think every hoop that every one must jump through should also apply. That way every one is truly equal.

Also I can not end this book with out revisiting what I said in the Welfare Trap. There should be a law that disqualifies any one who has been on public assistance of any kind from voting, until they have paid back what the Taxpayers have given them. Think about it, if your child who doesn't even pay rent starts demanding a say in how your house is run you would get rather up set. If someone who has no stock in a company comes to a shareholders meeting and starts to demand a say in how things are run, that person would be escorted out. So why does a person who has a proven track record of being a liability to the tax payer have a say in how things are run in America? Just something to think about.

In closing, I could have paid a narrator to do the task of turning "The Death of Democracy," into an audio book for me and I probably should have for the sake of quality, but I felt that you needed to hear the fact that I stutter when I read or even speak in public. I am blind and have many physical challenges that limits my ability to work, yet I go to work every day and have never missed any time at work. My wife and I pay our taxes and other bills with no help from anyone but God. Every one has their own disabilities, it is how or even if you choose to over come them that defines whether or not the government sees you as a Liability or an Asset. It is that choice not to feel sorry for yourself that determines if you will be assisted by a government who rewards people for complaining and penalizes people through taxes for becoming contributing members of society. Something is broken and the American people are the only ones who can fix it.

The Death of Democracy is the inspiring force behind the Si-Fi adventure series called The Agenda and a cookbook called the Urb an Cook, which teaches people to use what they have in the kitchen already, so they don't have to be swiping an EBT card. I would also like to point out to my readers that the precedent that was set by the Declaration of American Independence, was the successful separation from England: such a fact must serve as a reminder that no governmental power is absolute.

Please Note: This book is also found in Audio. All relevant citations, research notes, or journal entries, can be found in the companion book to this series, entitled: "THE ROAD TO SALVATION
RESEARCH NOTES, DAILY JOURNAL & BIBLIOGRAPHY FOR THE SERIES," IS FOUND IN THE FIRST EDITION OF THE NOTEBOOK MAGAZINE, AT WWW.OURCOMPANYPUBLISHING.COM.
THANK YOU FOR TAKING THE TIME TO READ THIS BOOK. UNTIL NEXT TIME, MAY GOD'S GRACE BE UPON YOU, AS YOU TRAVEL DOWN THIS ROAD TO YOUR OWN PERSONAL SALVATION.

ABOUT THE AUTHOR

Like most of us, Anthony and his wife Kansa struggle daily to make ends meet. However, Anthony continues to study his discipline, in spite of never knowing where their next meal is going to come from. You see unlike most Anthropologists, Anthony Antolic is a professional temporary employee. But don't let that fact fool you. Anthony's life experiences have left him with a keenly analytical mind, which he puts to use writing books that are meant to teach about God's place in our lives.

You can find The Road to Salvation Series at:
www.amazon.com/author/anthonyantolic

www.ingramcontent.com/pod-product-compliance
Lightning Source LLC
Chambersburg PA
CBHW072259310526
45795CB00012B/1871